WINDOW
SEAT

By Brittani M. Halliburton, Esq.

Window Seat
Copyright © 2018

Printed in the United States of America

DEDICATION

This book is dedicated to the girl that just wants to love and be loved.

CONTENTS

FOREWARD

During the middle phase of my life, God spoke to me, specifically about the middle and showed me how to crack my middle in a vision. He used the people around me and their responses to life to teach me a lesson on how to crack the middle. He filled my spirit to pen an open letter, this book, once I understood what was necessary to pull myself out of the middle I was in. So I pen this letter to those in the middle to let you all know that if you focus on the middle and appreciate your middle, I mean truly embrace where you are in life. Not looking to your left or right but literally blooming right where you were planted…it could lead to a beginning that will never end! I pray this blesses you as it has blessed me and inspires you to understand your middle. So that you can fulfill all there is to the life God has blessed you with.

> **"To those who feel like you are in the doldrums with no wind in your sails and that you're not getting anywhere, settle down. Everything is happening in perfect timing that you cannot understand yet. There are things that need to come into line with my plans and purposes**

before you can move forward, says the Lord. Be patient. Ecclesiastes 7:8 the end of a thing is better than its beginning; the patient in spirit is better than the proud in spirit."

We all have different dreams, goals, aspirations, likes and dislikes, struggles and issues; but there are some things in life that we all share in common. Those things are called the inevitable. Example, there is no one on this earth who can avoid aging. There is also no one on this earth who can avoid dying. The list could go on of things that we all must experience as a part of the inevitable. But instead of focusing on the big picture of the inevitable, let us spend some time cracking the codes in the middle of those inevitable situations.

I believe the middle of inevitable situations to be a phase in life that none of us can bypass. Whether that means you're in the middle of receiving an education, the middle of life happening, or the middle of your career. I like to refer to this time in life as God's grooming of character. This is a time where self-reflection will become a must, positive mantras are necessary, and turning a deaf ear to negativity will become a habit.

It is your time to grow. A time for your no(s) to mean no and your yes(s) mean yes. You will learn to find contentment in who you are and whose you are. Once the middle is over, you will know exactly what it takes to move forward, and every middle from then on will be celebratory. Now you may be wondering what I mean by "every middle." That's a valid thought. The middle, unlike death, is not indefinite. It is something that occurs with every "new" phase of life. Each "new" chapter you begin will have its middle, and that is what you will learn to take joy in. A new phase, new middle, new lessons, and new blessings. The middle is one of those things that once you've experienced it once you can pretty much grab a handle on how the process works.

THE EDUCATION

Often times in life, people find themselves impulsively excited about the beginning, sometimes considering the ending but never being mindful of the middle. There is so much excitement in the idea of starting a new job, going to a new school, or beginning a new relationship that as humans we fail to realize that we will all have to go through things once we cross the start line and begin the race.

Being taught throughout life to keep your eye on the prize, work hard in school, and finish with a high GPA to secure college scholarships is not as simple as it sounds. Work hard to secure college internships they say. Make good grades and graduate with honors they say. But it is not as simple as that. No one ever talks about the process of finishing high school and the road to college. The countless hours of studying, the application process, the lows and highs of being accepted by some colleges and rejected by others. No one warns you about the long research papers, the growling scheduling of classes, the joys, and fears of financial aid that all happen while in college.

Growing up as a child, I was always excited about school. I loved to read, and learning was fun to me. I was a part of everything, and I attended everything. By my senior year in high school, I was involved in so many organizations that I don't think I attended much school at all. However, all that excitement got me wondering what was next and how I could get there faster than the rate I was already traveling. So, I met with my school counselor. Before I knew it, I was registered for college courses and would be graduating a year early.

I finished high school at the age of 16 and enrolled as a freshman at the University of Louisiana at Lafayette at just 17 years old. I'd like to say; this is when I placed myself in the fast lane. I worked harder than I'd ever worked before to finish high school to get to the next point in my life. Looking back, I had no clue of what I was rushing off to. I was young and somewhat responsible, but I didn't know what I wanted. I barely knew who I was. But naturally, as a human being, I was looking for what was next as a lot of us all do.

I graduated college, and because I was so interested in what was next, I took a job out of state, immediately. Graduated, packed up and moved all in the same weekend. I got to my new destination and realized I was going nowhere. I was going nowhere fast. I suppose this was the beginning of my middle and 5 years later I am finally coming out. (MESSAGE: The middle isn't always short).

Some may ask. "Well, what job did you take? Was it your dream career?" Sadly enough, the response is a BIGG FAT NO! I took a job at a "marketing firm" that turned out to be a cold call/door knocking sells position. I quit on the second day and was forced to take a job I found listed on the green sheet to stay employed and keep my bills paid. What I did not understand about this time was that I was in the middle. I was going day by day just living and not giving any thought to where I was or why I was there, so it just seemed like life to me. And quite frankly, if I could get back to that mindset I would be forever grateful.

I never gave my middle any attention. I didn't sit and ponder on it. I didn't get lost overthinking in my thoughts of what I didn't have or what I wanted so badly. I just lived my life. Looking back now, no I wasn't rich, and I didn't have the best of things, but considering the mindset I would be forever grateful to go back. Your mindset is always a key factor in the middle. It determines the rate and pace you'll travel through the middle. I found that the more content I was the faster I climbed out. But the more I compared myself to others the longer the middle lasted.

I was content with what I had, who I was, and what I was doing. I wasn't bothered by what people around me had or what they were doing. I was focused on just living for me. I did what I wanted when I wanted, and I learn how to say yes when I meant yes and no when I meant no. I was independent and on my own with my earned education in tote. Finally, I got a call for a job interview that changed my life forever and opened up the doors to my destiny.

I began working as an administrative assistant it was my first salary job, and I was happy. After time passed with me being there, I found that with my surroundings changing my desires changed. I wanted more, and I wanted it instantaneously. I tapped into my childhood dreams of wanting to be a lawyer and applied to law school. After two years of working, I was a student AGAIN. This time I was a law student at Texas Southern University, Thurgood Marshall School of Law.

So I followed the pattern I finished high school a year early with a 3.8 GPA. I went to college at the University of Louisiana at Lafayette, finished got a job and made the decision to go back to school. But during all this time let me not fail to mention that I did not have the dream car or the perfect relationship, but it was in the back of my mind.

I use the phrase the "back of my mind" because as people as long as we are moving and making some progress even if that's wallowing in our own drama something is going on so the things we don't have don't seem so bad and there is energy being maintained in the middle.

And that's the first key to cracking the middle maintaining energy. However, you don't want to just maintain any kind of energy. You want to be sure to create and indulge in positive energy, a thought-provoking type of energy that will cause motivation to manifest within you. See I gave you my background to show you how casually living through your middle can get you by. But why just get by when you can excel and thrive by maintaining not just energy but positive energy.

THE EDUCATION ASSESSMENT

1. Top 5 priorities in my education

    _____

    _____

    _____

    _____

    _____

2. Top 5 fears/worries/concerns

    _____

    _____

    _____

    _____

    _____

3. Why am I afraid?

    _____

    _____

    _____

    _____

    _____

4. What steps can I take to disregard fear?

_____

_____

_____

_____

_____

5. How will I execute these steps of disregarding fear in my education?

_____

_____

_____

_____

THE CAREER

Graduate college and get a high paying job they said, but no one explains the job search, and how many times you'll be told no before you get an interview. There is no guidance or forewarning of what the job search can do to your confidence. No one shares the truth of how competitive the work force really is. It is a type of tough that if you aren't already feeling down about your middle it will take you straight to the bottom.

You want to get a great internship impress the company, firm, or partner and hope to be asked back consistently throughout law school until you graduate and they offer you a job.

All you have to do is work hard, study, visit the campus career counselors to have your resume reviewed, go through a few mock interviews to prepare yourself for the real deal, and you will get it. AANTTT WRONG! Well let me correct that all of those things are the necessary steps, however, sitting in orientation and hearing them compared to putting them into action are two different things.

And that my dear reader is the second key to cracking the middle, it is not enough to just hear the steps or discuss the options, but you have to get up and put things into action. If you want to succeed your middle and not get drowned by the thoughts of what you don't have and where you aren't yet in life you must be proactive.

Being in competitive environments can make or break us as people. They strengthen some of us and completely tear others apart. You begin to look at the people around you and desire more based on what they have and what they're doing a lot like I did when I started in the work field and was introduced to a whole new world. A world filled with name brand bags, shoes, fancy cars, and dinners out on the town constantly.

What we are unconsciously doing at this time in our life is creating our own middle and that my friend is the worst thing you could ever do to yourself. It's like you're defying the laws of gravity at this point. Life will inevitably give you a middle to every project, process, and phase of your life. But its, when you allow your thoughts to suffocate your sound judgment and jealousy of your neighbor surfaces things get chaotic.

I like to consider this going against the grain which means traveling in a direction different than that which God would have you and you land in the middle of self. Now you have to work and spend the time to pull yourself out, seek God, hear his voice and find the path you are supposed to be on.

Ultimately traveling around the mulberry bush when you were never intended to make that wasted trip.

1 Thessalonians 5:11

Therefore encourage one another and build each other up, just as in fact you are doing.

God does not make mistakes, and he has a purpose for you in everything he allows you to go through. He is also very particular about the people he allows you to go through things with. As people, specifically those in the middle have to find the joy in the middle and not miss the blessing of being in the middle so that we can use our middle to encourage someone else. The middle is ultimately a time to reflect on the beginning and make changes to perfect your character for the next beginning.

Some people would ask why aren't we preparing for the end in the middle? It's simple you are not preparing for the end because being in the middle is a phase and time of anticipation. You want to reach a higher level in something; you want more…you need more. You don't have to just wait until the end for such a large reward you look to the new…essentially the beginning.

I am certain that we've all at some point or another have heard the phrase "your attitude determines your altitude," or better yet patience is a virtue. But have you ever considered what those phrases mean to you and your middle?

Simply put waiting is deeper than just the act of waiting. It's largely about how you wait. When you learn to have an attitude of gratitude and wake up each day encouraged your wait begins to reflect a positive and productive wait, and your attitude begins to determine your altitude, and ultimately you are happier and more patient in your wait. Remember how you wait is key. How you handle your job that just might not be your dream job does not change the fact that; that dream may be crucial to your career path and be a stepping stone to where you are destined to go. So how you act on that job and treat individuals at that job is important. You should always be mindful of your actions.

My attitude truly determined my altitude. When I woke up excited about life and seeking ways to stay productive and living in a state of graciousness my altitude was much higher.

I was a much more pleasant person to be around. I loved more, I laughed often. I was able to give more of myself genuinely. The joy in my life spilled over into my career, and it was visible in my work product. I made new connections and beneficial relationships. I achieved more in the work day and I was recognized for my work. God began to open doors for me and create opportunities I would have never dreamed about. All because I had a positive attitude and my altitude was reaping all of the benefits as I went higher and higher in positivity.

It is very important that you don't just read the steps, but that you begin to take the steps. Being proactive is how you define your character in the middle. Don't get lost in self, fight and remain as grounded as possible. Work hard to not veer to the left or the right. Your path is yours, and no one else can define that for you and to look at someone else path won't help you figure it out either.

THE CAREER ASSESSMENT

1. Top 5 priorities in my career

   _____

   _____

   _____

   _____

   _____

2. Top 5 fears/worries/concerns

   _____

   _____

   _____

   _____

   _____

3. Why am I afraid?

   _____

_____

_____

_____

_____

4. What steps can I take to disregard fear?

_____

_____

_____

_____

_____

5. How will I execute these steps of disregarding fear in my career?

_____

_____

_____

_____

_____

THE RELATIONSHIP

"He or she is a great person," they say "you two should date"…"get married" yet no one discusses getting to know that person, learning to communicate and compromise with that person and the challenges of reaching a productive relationship with the goal of marrying.

We all like to bypass the middle and focus on the "prize," instead of being honest with ourselves and accepting that there is a middle and life is not a microwave dinner. It is important to understand where you are where you are going and that it is going to take time to get there.

What if someone told you there is a prize in the process? Would you be willing to slow down and smell the roses in the "middle"?

Let me be the first to tell you…there is a prize in the middle!!! You will become stronger, gain endurance, and learn tons of things you don't like before learning anything that you do like. But that's the prize, learning while in the middle.

You find courage and build character while in the middle, you learn yourself, and you learn things about people. The middle of a process can teach you how to handle situations in ways that best suit you. Ultimately assisting in your dating life. It is very hard for someone to get to know you when you don't know yourself. That's the fastest way to make your significant other feel less than and that the things they do for you are never good enough.

I am in a committed relationship yet I still have no ring and I am not engaged. While every holiday social media, emails, mailboxes and text messages are overflowing with pictures of love and invitations to weddings. It is very easy to get lost in your feelings of lack and to forget God's purpose for your middle.

As a little girl growing up the first dreams and fairy tales, we're often introduced to persuade us that there is a prince charming in the world that will come along sweep us off of our feet and we will live happily ever after. Briskly falling in love without even having time to think about what's next.

That fairy tale never mentions that sometimes you'll get the education, start the career and prince charming just might not be near. And that ladies, is the third form of the middle. You find yourself educated, content with your friends and family, you have your career, traveling and living the life you've always wanted yet prince charming hasn't quite found himself to be in the picture.

I myself have doubted my worthiness, and my ability to be loved. I mean face it sometimes the middle just outright does not add up. But the bible tells us in

Ecclesiastes 3:1-8

To everything there is a season and a time to every purpose under the heaven:

2. A time to be born, and a time to die; a time to plant, and a time to pluck up that which is planted;

3. A time to kill, and a time to heal; a time to break down, and a time to build up;

4. A time to weep, and a time to laugh; a time to mourn, and a time to dance;

5. A time to cast away stones, and a time to gather stones together; a time to embrace, and a time to refrain from embracing;

6. A time to get, and a time to lose; a time to keep, and a time to cast away;

7. A time to rend, and a time to sew; a time to keep silence, and a time to speak;

8. A time to love, and a time to hate; a time of war, and a time of peace.

And because that token is shared with us in the bible we should find peace and courage in our middle. Especially when you're doing everything you possibly can to be the best you. Lest we not forget we must know how to love ourselves, communicate and understand our feelings and be confident in our likes and dislikes before putting the time into understanding someone else's.

So don't get discouraged instead encourage yourself and speak positive vibes because there is a time for everything and everything has a time even in the middle.

I am a great example of prince charming being present, yet still not having the life you desire with him. Delay is not denial. We don't have the ability to know what is to come. However when things aren't panning out as planned I have learned you must try to be grateful. Have you ever stopped to think that if you received what you really wanted prematurely that you could cause damage to it? Or even worse you could lose it. All because the person you are isn't ready for something of that magnitude. So sometimes it takes a little more maturing before reaching certain points in life.

THE RELATIONSHIP ASSESSMENT

1. Top 5 priorities in a relationship

   _____

   _____

   _____

   _____

   _____

2. Top 5 fears/worries/concerns

   _____

   _____

   _____

   _____

   _____

3. Why am I afraid?

   _____

_____

_____

_____

_____

4. What steps can I take to disregard fear?

    _____

_____

_____

_____

_____

5. How will I execute these steps of disregarding fear in my relationships?

_____

_____

_____

_____

_____

THE WAIT

The middle of a situation, the middle of the day, the middle child…every middle has one thing in common…the wait. Waiting for the next beginning, the end, or the next best thing to come.

While experiencing the middle, you could become fatigue, ungrateful, impatient, unhappy, or even depressed, lost and angry. But instead of becoming those things speak life to your middle and get ahead of it. By embracing the middle and ask God what does my middle really mean.

Being in my mid-twenties, I am constantly surrounded by individuals experiencing brand new beginnings and middles, while I am also in the middle myself. I too have reached points of frustration, depression, and ungratefulness. But with God, I've learned to embrace what the middle means and was able to make my middle work for me and those associated with me. You see the middle is time to prepare you for your next beginning the person you were born to be per say. We can't say the end because the word (bible) tells us that no man knows the day nor hour that our king shall return.

Therefore, the perspective I like to take is that we are living from beginning to middle to beginning again. All the while trying to learn how to trust the process until the man upstairs says that it is finished.

It's a lot like driving around a city that is always under construction. People are quick to question when will all this construction end? Yet we never stop to think of all the construction our lives are under. We are all works in progress i.e. always under construction.

THE PROCESS

During the middle, you should certainly appreciate all that it has to offer. BUT always remember being in the middle does NOT necessarily mean it's just a time to wait. Your middle could very well be the pressure to transform you into the diamond you were destined to be. If you don't like your job, go out and create your own. Are you not satisfied with your relationships? Get out and start new ones. Pinpoint what exactly it is you are not satisfied with and get to work on changing it for the better. Remember be proactive.

It's all about learning yourself, appreciating who you're, where you're and grasping what your middle means. Let's face it we were all created different, and we all have our paths to take and with that comes several different middles.

The entire time I was in school I was looking forward to graduation. I just knew with everything inside of me that graduation would be my peak, and that I would move out of my closet sized room at my grandmother's house and I would get a Mercedes Benz and stop driving my 2008 yellow Pontiac. Yet things didn't work out that way because that was not the plan for the path I was on.

When graduation came and went, and I was still sleeping on my cot at grandma's house and driving my yellow Pontiac, it hit me. The time I should have been enjoying my middle, the time I should have been embracing the luxury of what my middle had to offer me I couldn't get past seeing what I thought would be a new beginning. Now you may have read that and thought luxury? Yep, luxury although I slept on a cot in what was basically a walk-in-closet I didn't have rent or utilities to pay. Although my yellow Pontiac was embarrassing it worked and I didn't have a car note. I was able to save more than I ever have, and that for me was true luxury.

After graduation I felt more defeated and caught in the middle than I'd ever been before, because instead of enjoying my middle as a student and preparing myself for what graduation would bring, instead of learning all that I could from my middle I hastily planned for the graduation. "The future" overlooking where I was and when I got where I was planning to be it was nothing like what I wanted.

So, maybe you're a recent grad, and you aren't sure what is next. Or maybe you just walked away from a job or unhealthy relationship. The first step is to understand that; that is perfectly ok. It is ok to take your time and smell the roses as some people say, while you are in the middle. It is even ok to not be ok. The middle is merely not being where you want to be when you want to be there. As long as you always gather all the pieces and keep on going it is going to be ok!

But if you sit and think about it the middle is a revolving door because once you reach one goal you'll be in the middle again trying to reach the next goal. So it is very crucial that as people we stop focusing on where we are and how fast we want to be at our next destination and that we begin to live and not just exist. In fact, as a recent graduate, new employee, newly single or just started dating, you're going to learn way more about what you don't want to do before you ever realize and commit to what you want to do. So take advice from someone that has been there…slow down. It's just another form of being in the middle, except this time it doesn't have to be disappointing because you will live in the middle and not just exist.

You won't allow your confidence to be shot, but it'll grow stronger. Jealousy will no longer have a place on your path but you'll celebrate in others keeping your energy positive. Competitive environments won't scare you and your gratitude will heighten your altitude.

THE TECHNIQUE

I'm an only child, but I've learned a lot about the middle just from being friends with people that are middle children. Middle children are often very in tune with their other sibling's needs, wants, and overall being. It is like growing up as the middle child you're naturally centered. I personally believe we could all take a page out of the book of a middle child.

They're typically the first to satisfy another sibling's needs or desires over their own selfish desires. In most cases they are OK with waiting for the parent to reimburse or compensate them for the love, care or attention that they gave to satisfy their sibling. It's almost as if it's a mindset that comes with being the middle child. Very similar to the mindset of the eldest sibling as a protector, the middle child can often be seen as the mediator.

Middle children seem to find peace for everyone and not complaining about the problem but working to solve it. They appreciate something about it and move forward.

Middle children often are less controversial than those that are only children or even the eldest of siblings. It is as if middle children are wired with a different understanding of where they are and where they are going. They're independent and unbothered by people thinking that they are walking in the shadows of their siblings.

They grasp the fact that although they are not the baby getting all the attention and not the oldest given most of the responsibilities they're still important. His or her role as middle child is pivotal to everyone around him or her.

As you go through this process called life and reach the middle of various situations and face the middle in numerous different forms never forget how pivotal the middle is to your success. The success of those around you and the success of those you are yet to meet.

Of course, it's your life and your middle so at any given time you can feel free to quit and not "wait around" for what the next beginning has to offer.

But why would you do that…you can't possibly think of one good reason you would stop the process you've endured this far, for a few months of fresh excitement starting from the bottom striving to reach the middle again? Not your best idea yet. So keep going.

No one ever said the middle was a race, and as individuals, we are under the pressure of the world we live in to keep up with those around us, or those that have "made it" in society better known as celebrities.

Ecclesiastes 9:11

I returned and saw under the sun that the race is not to the swift, nor the battle to the strong, neither yet bread to the wise, nor yet riches to men of understanding, nor yet favor to men of skill; but time and chance happeneth to them all.

God never intended for us to keep up with each other. But rather to live the life he's given us and seek his will in pursuing the life he placed before us. Our makeup and design was not for the world but to achieve a greater purpose that many of us still have not recognized.

Jeremiah 29:11

For I know the plans I have for you," declares the Lord, "plans to prosper you and not to harm you, plans to give you hope and a future.

While reflecting and learning to embrace the middle don't waste time. Get out try new things explore as much life as you can. Every day you open your eyes with warm blood in your veins you should do all you can to be happy for you.

You'll never realize how being happy for yourself can and will inspire someone else to be just as happy as you. Your middle could save someone's life right when you think the middle couldn't get any worst. And in that very moment, you could be facing your NEW beginning.

Moral of the story DON'T RUSH and DON'T GIVE UP!

As you have been reading, I'm sure it has crossed your mind of how to overcome the middle. Although we have discussed very critical keys to understanding how to live and not just exist in the middle. I do understand that you're human and you have more than likely been told your whole life to focus on the end goal. It is instilled within us to keep our eye on the prize naturally, so you're eager to learn how not just to crack the middle but overcome it.

However, Gods word tells us in Philippians 4:6 Be anxious for nothing, but in everything, by prayer and supplication with thanksgiving, let your requests be made known to God.

Use your time in the middle wisely, pray and seek Gods face in preparation for the next level. Don't allow your launching pad to frustrate you but instead when you feel dismayed and dazed pray. Talk to God about it.

Release stress and frustration in the most positive ways you know how. If that means to join a gym and workout, start researching the nearest gym now. Maybe you like to write purchase a new journal and log about your days and watch how God begins to make progress in your life.

Whatever it is that takes you to your happy place do that and work on becoming the best you. Remember the middle is a time of preparation it is not your permanent situation. Circumstances do expire.

God posed the question first in Matthew 6:27 when he asked can any one of you by worrying add a single hour to your life? Worrying about where you are compared to where you want to be or where you feel you need to be is not going to get you there. In fact it will slow you down. You'll find yourself spending too much time trying to figure things out.

Don't waste valuable time overthinking the process, instead trust God first and then trust the process. Relax and enjoy the opportunity to become greater than you already are.

Parents often teach their children that they can grow up to be anything they want to be, which is very true. Those same parents are infamous for admonishing their children by telling them this can be a good day or it can be a bad day you decide. Ultimately in both of those statements parents are teaching their children that you decide your fate. You can have a positive attitude about what is going on around you, and everyone can be happy, or you can be pouty, negative and create a bad atmosphere not only for yourself but those around you.

With that in mind, you're the master of your middle. You can be positive and use it to find the good in yourself. Or you can be negative and complacent never reaching the prize of the middle.

Someone might be reading this saying the middle sounds a lot like a catch 22 or a blessing and a curse.

Honestly, I couldn't agree with you more. But such is life; God created each of us with free will and the ability to make decisions. A lot like the way parents teach their children that they decide their own fate.

Some of us make what we feel are good decisions while others feel as though they couldn't make a good decision if their life depended on it. The point is there is no trick to life, and there is no trick to the middle. It is all about continuing to live in spite of, to remain hopeful always and never stop looking to learn.

Positivity is something that does not necessarily come easily to everyone. However, it is something that is easily rubbed off onto everyone. Prime example, it is hard to stay upset when someone is telling funny stories. It is also equally as hard to stay quiet in a room when someone is doing something wrong that you're knowledgeable and passionate about. It's like a fire inside of you that will cause you to offer help or advice on how to do it better. That's the power of positivity.

Finding what you love and doing it, staying busy (maintaining positive energy) and motivated. It is one thing that can help all of us through our middle. Have you ever stopped to realize the very things we worry about and allow to impact us negatively we don't ever think about when we are busy or when we are doing something that we love to do?

Why is that? Why does the middle not seem so bad when you're enjoying yourself or when you're so swamped and not have time to think about where you are compared to where you want to be? God shares with us the answer in

Proverbs 16:27-29

27 Idle hands are the devil's workshop; idle lips are his mouthpiece.

28 An evil man sows strife; gossip separates the best of friends.

29 Wickedness loves company—and leads others to sin.

Beat your middle by changing your mindset. Learn to not allow the dark thoughts of loud silence echo throughout your mind in down times and quiet times. Instead, enjoy the process, trust the process and work hard. Allowing yourself to become idle could cause more harm than you think.

Sitting at home being unhappy because you don't have the career you feel you deserve or terrorizing your own relationships because they aren't progressing the way you feel they should are all product of allowing your middle to overtake you. It can consume you and cause you harm.

If you know sitting at home alone is going to send you into a downward spiral of deep thought and sadness, invite friends over to play games, or watch movies. Go to the gym; go shopping find a book club and read. Expand your horizon and learn a new skill.

There are millions of things you can explore and spend time doing rather than digging a hole to push yourself into.

Sometimes it is as easy as opening your mouth while in line at the store talking to a complete stranger that can give you relief from your middle. You never know how someone may inspire and encourage you. Certainly you never know how your own story may be that encouragement for someone else. A kind word or a smile can go a long way when you're in the middle.

You don't know where you are going, but you do know exactly where you've been and the same God that brought you through the middle before is going to be faithful and just to bring you through again. Never let a temporary situation cause indefinite insanity.

As we journey through life, we learn a lot about who we are and who the people around us are. We learn to either respect each other's opinions or reject each other's opinions and continue to move forward. However, some of us have been guilty of rejecting others opinions and still not being able to move forward. Looking at the big picture, this is the process of creating perspectives.

One man may see a glass half full, and the other may disagree by saying it is half empty. You may be fed up with your "middle," but to someone else, you're just beginning.

Zechariah 4:10

the bible reads "Do not despise these small beginnings, for the Lord rejoices to see the work begin, to see the plumb line in Zerubbabel's hand."

This serves as confirmation that although you may not be exactly where you want to be, it doesn't mean you won't get there. You may not be enrolled in the four-year university of your choice, or have that car, or career or relationship but don't despise the small beginning because a delay is not denial. The fast track to success (should that even really exist) is not the destined path for all of us. You can probably think of someone that to you it appears they have it all and unbeknownst to you; you have no idea what they have gone through or what they are going through to be there.

Nonetheless, we all shall see success because success is measured by whatever you choose to call success. For someone getting out of the bed and starting their day is a success and they are rightfully entitled to that personal success.

As people, we have to stop comparing ourselves to each other. Comparing yourself to someone else will stifle your growth and suffocate your success, happiness and ability to thrive every single time.

"A flower does not think of competing to the flower next to it. It just blooms."

- Zen Shin

Create the life you want to have; by channeling positive energy and vibes around you and the people, you involve yourself with. Don't allow yourself to self-destruct. You were born to win and until you do you have to commit to working hard and not giving up on yourself.

You should be your biggest fan and if you aren't your biggest fan, we have work to do. If you don't believe in yourself who are you waiting on to believe? I won't wait for that response.

THE FIGHT

So now you've experienced a little excitement. You begin to see the light at the end of the tunnel just as you've begun to learn how to embrace your middle and maintain positive energy. You are content in your middle place. You're still dreaming about the end of the tunnel but you feel good…and the excitement begins to fade, but you aren't at the end of the tunnel. I like to call this the calm before the storm (the storm being your happy new beginning of course).

You've prayed…you've thanked God in advance and now there is silence. It is decision-making time. Will you continue to thank God, have faith and be at peace, or will you begin to question your faith and question if God heard you? Once again it is all about perception and choices. Happiness is a choice, patience is a choice, and kindness is a choice, in fact, living life is a choice. God is a God that gives you free will, which equates to choices. But what you don't have a choice on is Gods timing which is perfect timing. If we're just honest about it, Gods timing will mean you are ready and deserving.

It means you are well equipped and prepared for the new joys and challenges that are going to come with this new level. We have all fallen victim to say, "Nothing worth having comes easy." But so quickly do we all forget that saying when we are up against the hardest fight of receiving what we've longed for.

We've spent a lot of time discussing and breaking down different variations of the middle. From the good, the bad, the ugly but not everyone reading this is in the middle just yet. Some of you are at the beginning anxiously awaiting your middle because to you the beginning is not all that it is cracked up to be.

So what happens once you get the degree, the job, and the ring? You've changed your mindset, you are maintaining positive energy and your gratitude has taken your altitude higher than ever. Now it appears you have the life. But inside you feel you want more; you believe you deserve more. What do you do now? You work hard that's what you do. You get a pen and paper and create a vision. You make realistic goals for yourself, and you set sail on what is ahead of you.

Joy cometh in the morning...

I've given you all a brief overview of my wait throughout the contents of "The Middle." But what I did not fully share with you in this body of work is the faith that was born during my middle.

When God spoke to me regarding the middle; I was literally wallowing in my own distress. It took me almost a full year to find and match my faith with what God had for me. I prayed I fasted; I worked hard, I wrote my vision down and made it plain. But most importantly I trusted God blindly. I believed, and I knew that everything I wrote in my vision would align with his will for my life and come to past.

All glory be to God I received every part of my written vision not in my own time but Gods. Things I put dates on God showed up and made them happen before the date I prayed for.

The middle...the wait...the technique, the process and the fight is all about building your faith in God and becoming the man or woman he would have you to be. Always remember delay is not denial and when he says NO rejoice because that means there is a greater YES to come.

365 DAYS OF AFFIRMATIONS

1. There is nothing I cannot do.

2. I can do all things through Christ, which strengthens me-Philippians 4:13

3. I believe in me, and I believe in my ability to achieve everything I set out to do.

4. In all things we're more than conquerors-Romans 8:37

5. My foundation is strong, my heart is determined, and my mind is made up that I am worthy.

6. I have an abundance of reasons to smile.

7. I am a priority.

8. Today I will walk through life's open doors and receive positive surprises.

9. There is joy in every situation I encounter because joy is within me.

10. Today I will free myself by starting the day with forgiveness.

11. To have self-love is to have everything I could ever want.

12. I will embrace the free things in life today, breathing, smiling, and living.

13. I will commit myself to living life and will no longer just exist.

14. Jealousy is the root of all pettiness, and I will not let it consume me.

15. I will plant good in the world to reap good in my life.

16. Today I will pay it forward.

17. Be you because you are the best you.

18. Trust is a privilege.

19. My past will not control my present, and it will not determine my future.

20. There is no such thing as a small start there are only starts.

21. You can't run your best race looking behind you or on the side of you. You run your best race when you look straight ahead.

22. My success is measured using my own measuring stick.

23. Take the time to fall in love with yourself every day.

24. What you're going through will not break you because you were built for this.

25. Opportunity starts with you.

26. I love when you're happy. –Sincerely, self

27. Dear self, let's make today a great one.

28. Don't give up I'm depending on you.-With love, your future

29. The universe is cheering for me.

30. My creativity is unique and necessary.

31. My soul is a reservoir of happiness.

32. I deserve to be at peace.

33. Gratitude will start my day and joy will follow.

34. I appreciate change.

35. I will live at a pace that's best for me.

36. Striving to be better than I was when I started reading this.

37. The soundtrack to my life is peace, love, joy, happiness, and longsuffering.

38. Own your mental; you are a beast.

39. Keep your closet full, and your heart open.

40. There is no room for doubt in my life.

41. You only get what you give away so give love.

42. I am whole and healthy.

43. I have the perfect work-life balance for me.

44. I approve of who I am.

45. I am not afraid of the unknown because I was not born with a spirit of fear.

46. I listen to understand and not to respond.

47. Resistance is just life politely asking me to take a new route.

48. I embrace NO's because I know there is a greater YES ahead.

49. I am my greatest investment.

50. I find contentment in my alone time.

51. Loving myself is some wonderful.

52. The love story I have with myself is my favorite.

53. My dreams will come true.

54. Everything I desire will unfold before me in this lifetime.

55. I naturally repel drama.

56. I declare prosperity in my life.

57. I am a gift to those around me, and I am appreciated.

58. I am an important piece of the puzzle of life.

59. I am free, and my soul is blissful.

60. I can count on the people around me to hold me accountable.

61. Supporting others is healthy.

62. My needs are being met as I speak.

63. I have everything I need to succeed inside of me.

64. I have the power to become exactly who I want to be.

65. There is no such thing as a bad day as long as I am alive to see it.

66. I will let go of everything that does not make me happy and be completely happy about it.

67. I have created a clear-chartered path to a future filled with good health and wealth.

68. I will be considerate of my feelings and not let anyone get in the way of that.

69. I create healthy long lasting relationships.

70. I am a creative genius.

71. Good health, love, and prosperity are all around me.

72. My heart is mended, bigger than ever and open to new love.

73. I am not defined by what others think of me.

74. I will take criticism with a light heart and use it to my advantage.

75. I am living in the moment and enjoying everything that the moment has to offer.

76. I will not allow my life to be rushed instead I will enjoy it.

77. Downtime is a blessing.

78. I find comfort in silence.

79. The joy of the Lord is my strength.-Psalm 28:7

80. "My grace is sufficient for you, for my power is made perfect in weakness." Therefore I will boast all the more

gladly about my weaknesses, so that Christ's power may rest on me. - 2 Cor. 12:9

81. I am learning something even when it feels like I'm not.

82. God is preparing me for increase, and I can feel it.

83. Never pass up a chance to make someone else's day.

84. Forgiveness is key.

85. Live every day like it's the super bowl.

86. I am my only competition.

87. I will release my emotions in a healthy manner.

88. Sometimes it is ok not to be ok.

89. Always remember validation is for parking.

90. You are WOMAN, and you are WONDERFUL.

91. Trust the process.

92. I speak positivity into the universe, and it hears me.

93. Positive thinking will result in achievement of positive goals.

94. My goals will become my reality.

95. I am dependable.

96. Courage seeps through my pores.

97. Negativity is not allowed in my atmosphere.

98. I am aware of my needs.

99. Pain is weakness leaving the body.

100. My path is determined, and I acknowledge that it is positive.

101. Love surrounds me.

102. My joy is mine.

103. Today I will push me to be the best me.

104. Live everyday like it's a dress rehearsal.

105. I choose to give love.

106. Today I will walk in motivation.

107. The race is not given to the swift.

108. I am consistent.

109. Aiming high comes natural to me.

110. Beauty is my name and confidence exudes throughout me.

111. When the music stops I will keep dancing.

112. Success will come easy.

113. Financial stability surrounds me.

114. I find clarity in silence.

115. Me time is critical to my success and I will give me the best me I have today.

116. I will be understanding to those around me.

117. You have to play to win.

118. Wonderful positive surprises will find me.

119. I will live my dreams and not just dream.

120. I embrace change.

121. Circumstances expire.

122. Positivity is contagious.

123. Love is a way of life.

124. My surroundings will not limit me.

125. Today I will be the change I want to see.

126. I will express myself openly today.

127. The world is my playground and I shall explore all of its swings and slides.

128. Help of others is needed.

129. Because things are tough right now I will fight harder.

130. My life is an example of excellence.

131. I am more than a conqueror.

132. Life was designed for me to win.

133. My wings are spread, and my heart is open wide for change.

134. I love because I choose to.

135. My hurt cannot and will not define me.

136. I will make every day my best day.

137. I am strong.

138. I am surrounded by people that love me.

139. I will celebrate my life like every day is my birthday.

140. I will endure.

141. I am a champion.

142. I am woman hear me roar.

143. I am beautiful from my inside out.

144. Self-love is the most important love.

145. I will not allow others to determine my attitude.

146. I will not accept negative energy in my circle.

147. Today fancy will be my first name, and fun will be my last.

148. I am entitled to me time.

149. I will not feel guilty for walking away from things that do not push me, cause me to excel or make me happy.

150. Today I am starting my day in expectation.

151. Things will work out…they always do.

152. I wear confidence gracefully like a string of pearls.

153. It is ok to have standards. It just means I expect something out of life.

154. My life is a magnet for positive vibes.

155. I possess positive goals, and I am pushing for greatness.

156. Today I shall "get my life."

157. Good things come to those that wait…but better things come to those that grind.

158. I work to impress myself not others.

159. Things in life do get hard, but instead of complaining I will learn the patterns and create a plan of attack.

160. Today nothing will be able to stand in my way; I will walk in joy, speak in peace and operate in love.

161. I'm worth it, and I know it.

162. I will rejoice over the broken pieces of my life because they're being put together to make a masterpiece.

163. My goals will become reality.

164. Today I will sprinkle glitter on others and show the world love.

165. Even the sun still shines during the storm…so smile.

166. Embrace the free things in life.

167. Laughter keeps the heart light.

168. What will the easy things in life get you? Today see yourself one and take the challenge.

169. Love is but a try away.

170. It can't rain forever.

171. I am setting positive goals and pushing for greatness.

172. Change is welcome in my world.

173. My heart is my home, and my home is a safe place, and I will not allow things that are negative into my home.

174. I will practice patience daily.

175. Prayer changes things.

176. I am equipped to do everything God has planned for me to do.

177. Today I will give up on excuses.

178. Words have wings be sure that yours fly high.

179. Who's going to stop you...other than YOU?

180. Being lost is not always a bad thing... it's how new adventures are created. (You'll never explore new adventures if you always know where you are.).

181. Choose to walk by the golden rule.

182. Today let your inner child thrive, breathe, relax and enjoy the simple things in life.

183. Surprise yourself and spend time with you today.

184. In all things make love your foundation.

185. Desires are fun but try spending some time focusing on your needs today.

186. Never allow someone else's negative energy into your space.

187. Guard your heart, your mind and your pocket all with the same force.

188. Always take into consideration that plans are created to be altered.

189. Life's surprises are just a part of your destiny.

190. Appreciate who you are, where you are, and whose you are

191. Smile often, it's one of the things the government hasn't figured out how to tax yet.

192. Don't allow sleep to be the only time you dream.

193. Dedicate time for reflection to review where you've been and decide how you'll use where you've been to get where you are going.

194. Love is for everyone.

195. Motivation is motivation regardless of whom it comes from.

196. Wisdom isn't dictated by one's age.

197. Follow your heart regardless of what the road signs say.

198. Happiness starts with self.

199. Wear high heels and travel often.

200. The term "Perfect" is always open to interpretation.

201. The truth is powerful use it always.

202. Being honest with yourself is the first step.

203. Being grateful is just the half.

204. Taking the first step is always the scariest but standing still never cured any fears either.

205. The time it takes to smile is less than the time you're using worrying about it.

206. Don't leave you off of your list of things to do.

207. Encouraging others is sometimes the encouragement you need.

208. Soar above it all today.

209. Goals can be achieved faster than you think you just have to work towards them.

210. Dream BIGGER.

211. Understanding can take you a long way.

212. Find the necessity of self-judgment.

213. Jealousy is just untapped potential, exchange jealousy for confidence and tap into you today.

214. Laugh at yourself today you're funnier than you think.

215. The battle will prepare you for war fight wisely.

216. You can only control you.

217. Sometimes pain can be therapeutic use it to your advantage don't allow it to use you.

218. Flexibility is a must.

219. There is always going to be someone doing what you're doing the key is to always switch it up on them.

220. Confuse the naysayers.

221. There is nothing like a good challenge it makes the victory that much sweeter.

222. Nagging is a form of flattery.

223. Decide to let positive wildfires spread through your life.

224. Your life is a canvas, and you're the artist make it beautiful.

225. Support those that do and do not support you.

226. Own your mental.

227. You don't have to be a flower kinda girl to stop and smell the roses ever so often.

228. The good things in life really are free: love, hugs, smiles, air, peace, joy, kindness, and the list sort of goes on.

229. Wisdom doesn't always have to come with age.

230. Give it a try you just might surprise yourself.

231. Learning to appreciate the small things in life shouldn't be hard. Don't beat yourself up over it.

232. Greatness takes time, and success takes hard work. So put in the time and hard work to be a great success, it's within you.

233. No one ever won the championship by not getting in the game.

234. Knowing yourself should be a priority.

235. Cleansing your soul is just as crucial as cleaning your closet.

236. Act as you know.

237. There is no crash course in life so take your chances you can only learn lessons and create memories, either way, you live.

238. Go in with a positive frame of mind. It will save you in the end.

239. You only get one life to live make it good.

240. The most rewarding experiences involve using your gifts.

241. Effectiveness should be a priority.

242. Relaxation and separation are sometimes needs.

243. Be mindful of your surroundings.

244. Passion alone won't get you there.

245. At minimum try.

246. Make every shot your best shot.

247. Always give you your best, so you don't have to look to anyone else to give it to you.

248. Remember independence is a blessing and a curse.

249. Sometimes silence is wisdom.

250. Reflect on who you are and work on becoming who you want to be.

251. Don't rush yourself creativity and time go hand in hand the good things always take time to create.

252. Stand up for what's right even if you're standing alone.

253. Things are only as important as you make them evaluate your priorities today.

254. Your hands are only as clean as the towel you dry them on.

255. Always keep a no judgment zone.

256. Keep reality close and your dreams closer.

257. Readjustments are necessary.

258. Diamonds don't have to be a girl's best friend sometimes it's best that her goals are.

259. Some things shouldn't be left open to interpretation.

260. Don't just think you can...know that you can.

261. If you've read this far, you're doing GREAT.

262. Things are often only as complicated as we make them. Today take the time to simplify some things.

263. The things you dislike doing are always the hardest to do take it all in stride.

264. I'm going to be me because I don't have to be you.

265. Never forget that options are always available.

266. A clear mind should be as important to you as breathing.

267. You're closer than you think.

268. No such thing as a small step a step in the right direction is a step no matter the size.

269. Be your own silver lining.

270. Failure is just a launching pad for a new start.

271. Sometimes it takes the uncomfortable to push you to discover comfort.

272. Complacency is not your friend, but consistency is.

273. Why live a plain life when you can add color and sprinkles shine bright don't allow anyone to dim you.

274. Rest is LIFE.

275. A self-awakening is the best awakening.

276. Stop waiting until bedtime to dream.

277. Opportunity won't always knock first sometimes it'll just barge in, and you have to be ready.

278. Fun isn't just a thing of the weekend.

279. Remember love covers everything.

280. Endurance is a part of your DNA.

281. You will only get what you give, so give wisely.

282. Positive thinking is life changing.

283. Gratitude changes your attitude…like really it does.

284. Take your shot every day even if you don't think the ball is in your court.

285. Just make it happen.

286. Press your limits and try your luck.

287. No is not always a bad thing.

288. Love is a game, but life is the sport.

289. Never be afraid to take your talents elsewhere.

290. Location is everything.

291. A free mind is a necessity.

292. Your tongue is the strongest muscle in your body for a reason...be careful what you say.

293. Change is not a bad thing.

294. Think before you react there is often times a better way to handle things.

295. Today I decide never to neglect me again.

296. Always remember there are people and then there is you.

297. You are strong, you are beautiful, and you can do this.

298. Someone is always watching make sure you give them their monies worth.

299. Encourage yourself so that you're available to encourage others.

300. Don't wait for someone else to do it you thought of it make it happen.

301. Never forget the end is just the start of a new beginning.

302. Today I will not allow myself to feel bad about decisions I have to make for myself.

303. Living a healthy mental and physical life will be more than just a goal it will be a reality.

304. I will stop waiting for others to reward me and reward myself.

305. Victory is around the corner; you just have to keep walking.

306. Giving up is never an option.

307. Add to yourself today by supporting others first.

308. Learning to embrace your quiet time is one of the sweetest lessons in life.

309. Add a splash of color to your life canvas today; a smile is a good start.

310. Take a healthy stroll down memory lane and give yourself a pat on the back for the growth you've made.

311. Life takes people down different paths for a reason don't fight it embrace it.

312. Never fear sacrifice, instead hold it near and dear to your heart.

313. Remember, those closest to you may be the first to hurt you not because they don't love you but because they're standing to close to see you.

314. Step up and be the first to speak today.

315. Your mind is a gift but it's one you must control.

316. Life doesn't come with instructions so stop looking for them and just live.

317. Live a life so full of joy that you forget its Monday.

318. It's not just that good things come to those that wait, it is more so that good things just take time.

319. A well-rested mind is a good one.

320. Start your day expecting good news.

321. Hard blows are only to teach you your own strength so always fight back.

322. Even on a bad day, there is something to be grateful for.

323. Relax, relate, release

324. Life wasn't designed for you to win it was designed for you to learn.

325. Always keep your eyes open for the lesson.

326. Stop searching for opportunity and create it.

327. No one can stop you but you.

328. There are nice people in the world. Look in the mirror.

329. **The person you are looking for is in the mirror.**

330. Today find joy in the little things.

331. I will no longer allow someone else's measuring system of success rule the size of my success.

332. I am my own person, and I will respect myself as such.

333. Thinking out loud is healthy.

334. Choose to love yourself first.

335. Wake up and tell the universe what type of day you plan on having.

336. Loyalty will always be a part of my character.

337. I will not neglect my standards for anyone else desires.

338. I am stronger than most people think.

339. I will walk in freedom starting today, for the rest of my life.

340. I can only control me, the things I cannot change I will not allow to fluster me.

341. Confidence is in my genetic makeup.

342. Be the light you are searching the world for.

343. Someone needs you, remember him or her and keep pushing.

344. Always look for a chance to lend a helping hand.

345. Helping others is rewarding try it today and see what type of rewards come your way.

346. Hold your head up and walk in bliss you have that right.

347. Other people's opinions are just that an opinion.

348. Stare today in the face and say one of us must go down and it's not going to be me.

349. Live every moment as you'll never live in that moment again because you will not.

350. Every individual has a flaw you just have to embrace yours.

351. Living life in a judgment-free zone is the best zone.

352. Learning to let go may be a daunting task, but once it's done it's the most rewarding.

353. Start every day with love.

354. Forgiveness is only the beginning.

355. Sometimes taking things slow is necessary.

356. Learn yourself first…understanding who you are will benefit everyone around you.

357. When finishing what you've started becomes hard…remember why you started and worked harder.

358. You control the energy in your space be careful of who and what you let in.

359. You only get one life to live make it a good one.

360. The words like and love aren't interchangeable. Appreciate them both and their respective stages of life.

361. Vow to fill up for fun while you can.

362. Your life was tailored just for you wear it like it's going out of style.

363. Being there for others is sometimes the least you can do.

364. Stop allowing the things you cannot control, control you.

365. The person you are looking for is within you.

WORD OF THE WEEK

Growth- Walk in this week accepting personal growth. No matter how big or small that growth is take pride in it for you. Embrace the learning lessons and celebrate your victories. Don't allow anyone around you to challenge your growth. Only you know where you have been and where you plan to go. Breakaway from comparisons this week you are your biggest competition lets be better than last week and work on growing. GROWTH!

WEEK 2

Increase

Whatever it is you're working on work harder. Smile more, love often and watch the increase around you. Don't be afraid to speak up this week. Take on the new challenges and wear increase like a crown of sunrays. Losing a few hours of sleep to put in overtime on your dreams will be rewarding.

WEEK 3

Love

Without love, we're nothing at all. God showed us the greatest love of all by sending his son Jesus Christ to die on the cross. Spread love and watch how it's reciprocated. Open your arms, heart, and mind to someone new, or reach out to someone old. Don't allow hurt or disappointment to stop you from sharing love.

WEEK 4

Forgiveness

Forgiveness is the key to life. It's the only freedom you can afford yourself that will buy you a rich future. Forgiveness shows maturity and respect not necessarily for the person you forgive but respect for yourself. It shows that you love yourself too much to allow someone else to hold you in bondage. When we don't forgive we can't walk around with a clear conscience. It's hard to move forward and make self-progress when we hold hatred and anger in our hearts towards other people. Fight negative thoughts, actions, and reactions with forgiveness.

WEEK 5

Patience

Patience is a virtue, and whoever came up with that saying should receive a gold medal. Patience is grueling, hard, frustrating and time-consuming. BUT once achieved it's rewarding, life-changing, and worth the wait to say the least. This week let's wake up thankful, put a smile on and wear patience as a jeweled crown. It's your accomplishment, and you deserve to walk in its glory. So you might be reading this saying yea patience sounds good and this is an encouraging read, but what are the steps to achieving this "patience." I'm so glad you asked. Say this prayer with me if you will "Lord I surrender my thoughts, actions, and fears to you. I ask that you take control of my being and guard my heart. When frustration attempts to come upon me, I ask that you speak to me and direct my ways. I give you control, and I accept your will. Amen." Now walk in patience in this day and watch as the blessings of patience unfold before you.

WEEK 6

Obedience

The word of God tells us that obedience is better than sacrifice 1 Samuel 15:22. We all have what we consider to be intuition in moments when we are unsure of what to do or how to handle something. But sometimes we should remember that the small voice of reason you are hearing is God heeding you to the fact that obedience is better than sacrifice. However, in those moments when you aren't sure of the next step to take, say a quick prayer for guidance so that you can heed the direction of the Lord and not get lost in your own way (a.k.a. flesh). Battling whether to let that "thing" go or to leave and walk away without looking back listen for a word from God. Obedience will open doors in your life that will lead you to a fulfilling God willing and God timing life that will be full of joy and positivity.

WEEK 7

Compassion

We all have our days when we could use a little compassion, and we've all been in that place where the random "how are you" message from a friend means more than they could imagine. Be that compassion for someone this week. Pay it forward, hold a door open, share a kind word with someone, or stop by and visit your family. Compassion is a lot like love, you get what you give so choose to give compassion.

WEEK 8

Strength

You never know how strong you are until being strong is your only choice. I've often heard people say God gives his hardest battles to his strongest soldiers. This week wake up boldly and take pride in your strength. Surprise yourself and go a little harder, work a little longer. Like all character traits, you have to work with them to perfect them and finding strength is no different. Pushing yourself is no longer an option but a requirement.

WEEK 9

Positivity

Positivity is one of those things that is infectious and can spread like wild fire if you just take the lid off. Turn that frown upside down and close the door to negativity. Positive vibes only all week long, the true test will reveal its self when you have to shy away from those you love to protect your positivity. Battle them out and speak positivity openly about their lives. Let your light shine nothing but positive vibes.

WEEK 10

Peace

Peace should be the one thing in your life that is never up for negotiation. There is no give and take when it comes to your peace, guard it with your life. This week explore your peace and find new ways to enhance your levels of peace. Go to that place that only you and your mind enjoy. The place where you don't have to entertain anyone else you don't have to please or answer to anyone else. Try practicing your peace in the middle of a crowded room. At that point you have maximized and mastered your peace experience to its highest heights. Enjoy!

WEEK 11

Endurance

Endurance is a lot like strength and patience. It's tested just as often but it can be tamed and increased. You can do it! This week face those fears and put your troubles behind you because you were built for this. Endurance is but a piece of cake, and you are about to blow out the candles. Enjoy the sweet victory of enduring what everyone around you thought you couldn't.

WEEK 12

Motivation

Motivation- The same advice, encouragement, and motivation you found yourself recently sharing with that friend or family member…take heed to it this week. Motivation starts at home. If you can't motivate you what exactly are you waiting for someone else to say or do? How are you expecting this person to touch home for you if you haven't learned how to touch you? Get excited about who you are this week and what you are capable of. Not what someone can say to you that sounds good. But what about yourself that can get you going. Be your biggest motivation this week.

WEEK 13

Ambition

Ambition is a necessity borderline requirement. If you're ambitious or you aren't quite there yet no worries, we have the whole week ahead of us to work on our ambition. Start by figuring out what inspires you, what makes sparks and butterflies fly within you. Set aside sometime this week to journal and work through your thoughts on what ideas you have that you could talk about or write about all day and all night long without a break. Those are the very things that you're ambitious about. Let your ambition shine it's in there you just have to work with it.

WEEK 14

Success

It is one of those things that's measured by every individual rightfully, like the phrase "to each its own" to put it simply. The key to success, however, is to understand the difference between competition and jealousy. Jealousy, on one hand, will suffocate success because you'll be blinded by those around you and what they are accomplishing or not accomplishing compared to yourself. While competition can be friendly and motivating to an extent. This week measure your success choosing whatever metric system you desire. Not looking to your left or right but straight head in the mirror at yourself. Take success head on.

WEEK 15

Opportunity

As long as you're living, willing and able there is an opportunity. You disagree? Wonderful I'm glad that you did because if you don't believe that there is opportunity surrounding you every day all day that means you need to get out and create opportunities for yourself and those around you with like interest. This week map out possible opportunities and give them a shot. But while mapping out those opportunities take some special time to evaluate what you can do to help yourself better and create paths of opportunities for yourself.

WEEK 16

Jealousy

Jealousy this has to be the ugliest trait known to humanity. This week it is our task to work diligently to break free of it deceiving and heart wrenching chains. Find your freedom this week fight against its forces by doing the unthinkable. Spread compliments instead of gossiping. Change your altitude and help those around you rise to new heights by allowing your positive good spirits to rub off on them.

WEEK 17

Hatred

Hatred is vicious and comes in several forms but it's your task to recognize hatred this week and flee. Hatred is one of those things that grows and seeps into our pores over time. Often it's unknowingly and triggered by someone hurting you first. But this week let's try adulting and being mature about situations of the past or those that offended us. Let's dig deep into why we feel the way we feel and consider the intentions of all parties involved. Let's grasp a new perspective and let go of hatred for good.

WEEK 18

Self-Doubt

Self-Doubt is your worst enemy. It holds you back with greed, and it swallows your confidence like a raging sea. Pull out of the dump of self-doubt this week by declaring to yourself that you're more than a conqueror and that you will achieve every thing you set out to do. Now grab your pen and pad and set your goals out clear and straight. You are a shooting star now take off from your launching pad and shine for the entire world to see. Someone is in need of what is inside of you, so share.

WEEK 19

Trust

It only takes one time for trust to be broken and for some reason, it appears trust is gone and destroyed forever. Maybe because it is complied of several tiny pieces that create a beautiful masterpiece, like a mirror and once shattered it's hard to see clearly of where each piece came from to put it back together again. You walk around paranoid watching your back and living with caution tape wrapped around you like a cocoon. But what if you broke out of that cocoon and accepted that whatever was done to break your trust is not your fault. Nor the fault of those around you that you are not willing to give a first shot at trust. What if I told you the way to truly heal is to air that wound out. By speaking about your hurt, to share it with others clean your wound and trust again. Learning to trust is very similar to learning to ride a bike. You're bound to fall, scrap your knee and even cry. But you get up, try again, and eventually, you get the swing of it. So this week work on getting up, trying again and eventually you'll be in the swing of trusting again.

WEEK 20

Self-Control

Self-Control is something that can benefit you and everyone around you. It creates maturity and shows elevation in your life. It's more than knowing when to walk away or when not to respond, but it's that restraint that keeps you from stressing out over your inability to control other people. It restrains you from going crazy on the individuals that are driving you crazy because you can't control them. Self-control is like walking around in a bubble and avoiding negativity and drama with a pocket full of sunshine playing in the background. Today, jump in your bubble and jam out as you practice self-control.

WEEK 21

Passion

Ever wondered what passion really is? Or maybe you've wondered how you know if you have a passion for what you're passionate about. Example, have you ever had an idea to do something or create something and just the thought of the idea got your heart racing, and you felt warm inside like a jar of butterflies were released inside of you? You just jumped up and started jotting those thoughts out and couldn't stop smiling or thinking about that idea? In fact, you're smiling right now reading this because that idea instantly came to mind. That's passion it comes from deep within you, and no one and nothing can stop you from achieving the end goal. You're willing and ready to do anything necessary to get it done, and you most certainly will get it done. Hop out of bed this morning and chase that passion. Remember there are 24 hours in a day and you must give that passion at least 1 each day.

WEEK 22

Dedication

It's that important character feature that we all encounter at one point in life or another. Whether it's exposed to our work ethic, educational career, personal relationships, or just self-commitment it can make or break things we experience in life. Dedication is often tested and births other character traits within us like loyalty, love, and inspiration. So live out your commitments and show dedication this week. You never know where it might take you.

WEEK 23

Kindness

God loves kindness, which is exactly why kindness should be a priority of ours. We live out each and every day of our lives experiencing a kindness that we don't always deserve. Yet we walk around like being kind to others is an option. If it's not our family or friends, we sometimes feel that there is no obligation to be kind. Take a moment and think about how different the world would be if we all walked around in kindness. Kindness is as simple as holding the door open or saying thank you when a total stranger opens or holds the door open for you. Saying hello is even an expression of kindness. It goes a long way and can be life-changing. Let's share kindness this week please. See I just exhibited kindness by simply saying please at the end of my statement. Never forget, your actions are always being registered in memories and impressions.

WEEK 24

Listen

Listening is a very crucial and detrimental to communication and the activities associated with communication. But many of us live each day only listening to respond. When someone starts talking naturally our minds are in thinking mode to respond and have an answer for whatever it is that's being said. I challenge you this week to listen for the benefit of hearing. Hearing out what the person has to say, what they're feeling and hearing how you can better assist or react to your response after fully listening and hearing the person out. Master the art of hearing and see how it enhances your levels of communication. Ready...set...Listen!

WEEK 25

Courage

Courage is something that's often taken for granted and overlooked. It's one of those things that we all want, need, and have at different points in life. But we as people never fully reward ourselves for standing up and finding our courage in situations. When if we took the time to be proud of our courage when we use it, I believe it would be a lot easier to locate it when it's necessary. Have you ever found yourself standing up for someone else? If the answer is yes, and I'm sure that it is, that took courage, but I'm also sure you didn't stop and recognize the courageous act you performed. But when it comes to standing up for yourself you aren't so sure where your courage is hiding, and it's hard to stand up and bolt out that courage. With that being said I challenge you to a game of courage this week. Not for anyone else but for yourself. Stand up on that job and speak what is true, stand up in that relationship. Take control of your surroundings this week! Be courageous.

WEEK 26

Fear

Like love, sadness, excitement, happiness, joy, and nervousness, fear is just an emotion. It's what we tell ourselves and accept as the truth and allow it to hinder us from living and thriving in life. Some call fear the unknown. It creeps in when you don't know what to expect, but I say let's give fear the boot and when we found ourselves in those unknown situations lets approach them with positive emotions. Accept happiness, joy, fun, and excitement as the truth. Take a step away from the wall and leave fear hanging on it. You shall live a life of fulfillment and fear is not allowed.

WEEK 27

Balance

Balance is a necessity that as human beings we shy away from because of responsibilities and obligations. We work hard all week chasing the weekend and collecting a check to pay bills. Never stopping to realize that not even for 30 seconds did we lie in bed and just breathe. When the alarm goes off, we jump up starting our days rushing to get out of the house. This week I challenge you to stop running, working, splurging on the weekend and repeating. I challenge you to take time in the mornings and time at night to enjoy the simple pleasure of yourself. Whether you spend that time reflecting and making a journal entry, praying, listening to music, or if you just want to sit in silence. Take that time for you so that during your run, work, splurge routine you don't run into confusion, exhaustion, and frustration. It's all about balance appreciating yourself and stepping away to show yourself how much you do appreciate yourself. Carve out some balance time and add balance to your routine, it's worth it!

WEEK 28

Organization

For some, it comes easy and for others not so much. For some its second nature and they can't function without it, while others find it tedious and seek the thrill of flying by the seat of their pants and shy away from the restriction it creates. Whichever side you may be on lets first start by saying you aren't wrong you have found and appreciated what works for you. Secondly you function through organization because organization is all about perception. There is no right or wrong way to do it. It's merely learning how you best get it done and sticking to it. Being organized and exhibiting organization is more of a "to each its own" type of principle. The goal of organization is really and truly sticking to it. Creating a way to work through something and using that method consistently. Moving forward embrace your version of organization it is what's keeping you afloat so if that means coloring outside the lines you color on. And if it means tracing the lines and staying clean and fine within them trace and stay within. Now let's show the world the many forms of organization and change a few things while we're at it.

WEEK 29

Time Management

We've all lived in the moment where we are either telling ourselves that we need a work/life balance or we have been in the position to be told. Work/life balance is crucial to your well-being for more than one reason. However, creating and maintaining this balance can only be developed through proper time management. Proper time management starts with being very specific regarding your needs for the day followed by your desires. Needs and desires in your work life should be written down strategically to ensure that each work day gets you closer to the desired end of the next day and project. For instance label each work goal by Roman numerals followed by letters that break down what it takes to achieve and complete the task listed under each Roman numeral, very similar to creating an outline. After you've completed your work to do list create a personal list with at least 3 things you will do for yourself or with friends and family to ensure you balance the time you spend in a day. Once you've properly mapped out your to-do list time management really kicks in. First and foremost complete each work task on the list daily. Try your best to avoid task from your list lingering on to the next day; second don't allow work task that is not on your list overtake you and trump your personal to do list. Now, realistically speaking everyone experience's work emergencies and cant avoids things popping up, BUT that means you must work harder to achieve everything set out for the day. You shouldn't have to let your personal list down because work duties called. Sometimes it's helpful to even set alerts and alarms on your phone when you start a certain task to ensure you don't work overtime on one thing and that you keep a consistent flow throughout your day. Once you've mastered time management, the work/life balance will be a breeze. Be upfront with others about your time trust me you will thank yourself for it in the long run.

WEEK 30

Priorities

Priorities much like goals should always remain near and dear to your heart. Priorities are the things in life that you cannot afford to avoid and avoiding them usually create problems you don't want. Organizing your priorities are key to seeing each of them get the respect and time necessary to see them through to completion. Although priorities are known as things that are of more importance than things you handle daily, it is possible that you have more than one priority at a time. It's important you can distinguish between what is most important and what can be done second all while keeping in mind that all of your priorities need to be addressed in a days' time.

WEEK 31

Expansion

Expansion starts with a grateful heart, faith in yourself, confidence and a dash of expectancy. Being grateful for where you are in life and what you have in life, enough belief in yourself to expect more of yourself, confidence that you can and will achieve expansion and the drive to work harder and push yourself (a.k.a your dash of expectancy). With those gems in tote, expansion is bound to come your way because you will overflow and burst out of the realms in which you are living. Your grateful attitude will cause your hard work to be genuine and natural. Working in your natural glee will allow your dash of expectancy to flow and bring flavor to your work confidence. Befor you know it that promotion you wanted on your job will be yours, those A's you wanted to make on your exams will be yours. The world will open its doors and expand its land to you freely.

WEEK 32

Self-Love

Self-love is a one of a kind love it's the most important and the most sincere form of love you will ever experience. The love you share and hold in your heart for yourself is powerful and determines what you accept from others. It's an open and honest love because let's face it you can't hide anything from yourself. You know your heart and intentions in everything you do. Self-love is so meaningful and electric that if you don't have self-love running through your veins, it is hard for you to have any other type of love. In fact, understanding or being open to accepting love from others is impossible when you do not have true self-love. I say that because if you don't see you as worthy to be love you won't see and accept someone loving you. Let's start this week by telling ourselves how much we love ourselves and continue to spread that love throughout the week. Each time you pass a mirror take a moment to say, "I love you simply."

WEEK 33

Joy

Joy is when you become a part of the true winner's circle. Joy is never ending and purely rewarding. It is far more valuable than happiness and surpasses contentment. People around you can't give it and they can't take it away.

WEEK 34

Confidence

Confidence can be groundbreaking and earth shattering when worn correctly. Confidence worn graciously adorns you like a crowned halo of fresh glow. It is within every one of us, we are born with it. However, as we grew up mature and began to take the blows life throws our way we tend to allow our birth given confidence to be hidden. And in moments like that you literally have to work like a mad woman or madman to find it again. It's one of those things that you can never quite give up on because it's such a necessity. So this week let's not give up on our birth given right of confidence but let's fight to find it and live in it.

WEEK 35

Respect

Of course I could start out with a cliché line about how respect is earned not given, but have you ever considered giving respect first and watching it be reciprocated. Just like any other form of positive energy you put out into the atmosphere. We were all placed on this earth to love each other regardless of anything else that may or may not happen. We were placed here on a duty to love ultimately equating to exhibiting respect for everyone. Just because someone isn't showing you respect or has disrespected you doesn't give you the green light to disrespect him or her back. Respect is a standard that we have to be mindful to first hold ourselves to before we can expect the same from others. This week take a look in the mirror and ensure the person looking back at you is showing respect. Before you point fingers at someone that might not be so respectful.

WEEK 36

Humility

Humility-people tend to not give the character trait of humility the praise it deserves. Humility is one of those traits that teach you wisdom and create loyalty amongst you and the crowd. When executed it screams adulthood, self-control, and wisdom. Sometimes humility is looked down upon because if you find yourself going against a certain beast, it could be equated to turning the other cheek. But what is it about turning the other cheek that we as humans look down and frown upon it. Who are we to exhibit such snooty behavior…when we all need to exercise humility? This week, walk in humility in every situation you can. Watch how powerful you feel just by showing humility.

WEEK 37

Loyalty

Some people long for it and some people demonstrate it so much that think of it as a catch 22 because sometimes you may be a person of loyalty yet a person longing for it at the same time. But that's ok, don't allow others lack to slow you down or deter you from being the person you are. The best-taught lesson is one by example. Continue to lead and show loyalty to everyone, even those that aren't always so loyal to you. Their time will come around, and it'll surprise you both. Loyalty is a game of longevity it's not the first one to show it, but who can be consistent and never stop showing it. Don't count everyone out just yet.

WEEK 38

Clarity

Clarity is much like the difference between life and death. One wrong interpretation, or one decision to not ask a question further in detail, and you can be on your way to a whirlwind of negative energy. But taking the time to go the extra mile and achieve clarity before ending a conversation can open up a highway of peace and positivity. Clarity has a way of giving you a new walk and shedding new light on old thoughts. Take a step back this week reflect on conversation and get the other person involved. Clear up what you misunderstood, ask what they really meant by that. A bit of clarity will give you life. Try it!

WEEK 39

Sacrifice

Sacrifice there is nothing quite like a good sacrifice to get you going. A good sacrifice is like a sweet aroma before a fresh start. It is when you dig down deep inside of you and allow the feelings, concerns, needs, and desires of others to thrive before your own. Sacrifice permits you to feel proud and accomplished when you achieve what you have always had your heart set, on because you were bold and mature enough to deny yourself to receive something greater later. However, the key to sacrifice is to just trust the process. It won't always feels good, it's going to get tough, and at times you will want to give up. But hold fast and keep going because no sacrifice has ever gone in vain.

WEEK 40

Gratitude

Gratitude defines your altitude I'm sure we've all heard that phrase at some time or another. But imagine if we all lived by that phrase instead of just being familiar with it. I challenge you that for the next week to live, eat, and sleep gratitude. Watch the positive life-changing impact something as small as being grateful for all five senses will make. Remember there is nothing too great or small to be thankful for. So let's put on a smile and just be grateful for it all.

WEEK 41

Productivity

Productivity can be measured in several ways. Society will tell you what is acceptable and what the most respected levels of productivity are, and that's fine, but you have to remember the most important way. Productivity is measured by what you think, believe and desire of and for yourself. I tackle each week by writing out my to-do list and goals for the week on Sunday and every day at the end of each day moving forward through the week, I measure my productivity by what I was able to complete that day. Anything I did beyond my list is bonus productivity and a reason to call myself Super Woman. So let's get producing Super Woman.

WEEK 42

Faith

Faith, the substance of things, hoped for…the solid foundation we must all stand on. Faith is a necessity much like air and water. I challenge you this week to walk 100% in faith. To blindly trust and believe that the things you are working and building towards in your life will come happen for you. Although that is easier said than done give it a try. Having faith is a huge stress reliever. The time you take worrying about things can't change or fix any situation. So let go and exercise faith. It'll work out.

WEEK 43

Laughter

Laughter is free, contagious, and heartwarming. Something we all can afford to do more often without losing anything. It's used to lift spirits and hey sometimes if you do it hard enough you could shed a few pounds. It's fun, it's silly, it's refreshing and invigorating to say the least, and it fills rooms like a candlestick and warms hearts like a fireplace. Forge forth this week in laughter in the face of negativity, fear, and confusion. Laugh because those things do not signify the end. Don't sweat the small stuff. Cool it off with laughter.

WEEK 44

Acceptance

Acceptance is something we have all dealt with or avoided in some fashion or another. But instead of looking at acceptance from the point of view that we all know too well (others accepting us) let's look at acceptance from the point of self-acceptance. Accepting who we are and not being afraid to share who we are with the world. Accepting our flaws, our positive traits and our not so positive traits. Only until we fully accept ourselves will we be able to accept others and accept others as they have accepted us. Acceptance starts at home try it out.

WEEK 45

Meekness

Meekness is sometimes mistaken for weakness. But to be a good leader, you have to know when to follow. A good leader encompasses meekness as a character trait. Knowing when to speak and when to listen. Respecting everyone and their position and opinion on things. Meekness is a sense of awareness. Knowing who you are and not allowing anyone else to jeopardize or make you feel insecure about who you are, and what you stand for. Meekness is a lesson we can all benefit from, start this week with meekness and allow it to become a habit.

WEEK 46

Accountability

Accountability is something we could all use at some point or another. It's that extra push that's necessary to reach our next goal. It could be a weight goal, to finish reading a book, or writing a paper. It's the drive we all have deep within us, but it takes someone else to wake it up and say hey I'm watching you and holding you to this. Accountability is one of those things that just works best when there is more than you involved. I not only challenge you, but I encourage you to find an accountability partner to hold you responsible. Find the accountability within yourself to uphold someone else responsible. It's the "you scratch my back I scratch yours" scenario so that we all win.

WEEK 47

Support

Support is detrimental to our health, mental and physical. But if you aren't careful support can lead you down the wrong road and lead you down that road quick. You may read this thinking what is she talking about. Well, like most things in life there is a positive and negative to support. True supporters will tell you when you're wrong just as quickly as they would tell you when you're right. While naysay supporters will be a yes man, agree with everything you say and do. Yet the moment something goes wrong they'll jump ship and talk about you like they were just steering your sail. However, discuss positive support a bit more it's something we all need and without it we can suffer mentally and physically. So take a stand and support that friend you saw doing something amazing on social media, or sign up to be that volunteer and support a good cause. You never know when you'll need the support back.

WEEK 48

Self-Truth

The truth hurts this is true. But the truth is one of the healthiest serums you could feed anyone. Something even healthier than the truth is self -truth. It requires a lot of you but once you reach a self-truth the sting of the truth from others is lessened. In self-truth you find acceptance, you reach explanations and understanding about who you are. You realize who you are trying to be and what it's going to take to get there. But more importantly what changes it will take to get there. Self-truth is awakening and refreshing, a sign of maturity, and growth from the inside out. Before we divulge in serving others the truth, let's fix up a nice dose of self-truth this week and dine from our own kitchen.

WEEK 49

Creativity

Creativity is a gem in the jungle, an oasis in the desert. It's mystical and magical and sheds a part of itself within all of us. Creativity is the freedom to be yourself, yourself as in who you are when the doors are closed, and the lights go down. It's the songs we make up in the shower and the poems we create when we doodle. It's the voice that talks to you when color schemes and shapes stand out. It's a driving force in society. There is no such thing as weird or weirdo's; there is only creativity and creators. Creativity tells you to color outside of the lines and its ok, it tells you to mix that pattern with that solid and go outside to take on the beautiful day. It drives you to be you, so live outside the lines moving forward and see what beautiful mess of creativity you compose.

WEEK 50

Silence

It's amusing that the golden rule is to treat others the way you want to be treated…and to add to that if you don't have anything nice to say don't say anything at all. With the key phrasing being "don't say anything at all" because silence is golden. Often we think the most effective way to get our point across is to verbalize our feelings, and use expressions to communicate and share what we think. When really sometimes silence is the most powerful tool we can equip ourselves with. It gives you and any other party involved time to reflect on what has happened, and create a plan of action or suggestions on what should happen. Really, to just be frank sometimes silence saves you a world of trouble, hassle, and fights. Stepping back and sitting silent can move mountains that you thought the sound of your voice could crumble. The next time you find yourself in a tizzy sit back and let silence fight your battle. You might be surprised how quick the white flag is waved.

WEEK 51

Generosity

When done it can change a person's entire universe. When ignored and not shown it can burn a person's universe. It's powerful and important for success in life. Being generous and exhibiting generosity to those you know and love is wonderful. It makes you feel good, it makes the receiving person happy, but there is nothing like entertaining a stranger with generosity. That's when the true power of generosity is ignited. Holding the door open for someone, or saying thank you to someone that held the door open for you are the smallest steps towards showing generosity to those outside of your circle. Create positive energy for others to feed off of by being generous and showing generosity. You never know who you might meet or whose life you might change. Give it a try.

WEEK 52

Lost

I was once the girl that was lost. I'm sure I'm not the only girl that has been lost. Nor was I the only girl lost at the time. But when you're lost you can't see the others around you, you don't hear them; you don't even feel their presence. You're lost in the world, lost in your thoughts, lost in the pain that you're allowing to suffocate you. But what I learned about being lost was that even though I cried, even though I was sometimes scared I learned who I was. I came out knowing how to say no; I came out knowing it's okay to do things alone. Sometimes you need that alone time for just you, to simply love on yourself and engulf yourself in the essence of yourself. Everything about being lost isn't bad. Hold your head high even if you are lost you won't be lost forever. And hey! Even if you don't find your way, "home" or what you think is "home" keep an eye out for the new place God might have in mind. Being lost is an adventure that if you don't embrace it, you'll miss it.

www.ingramcontent.com/pod-product-compliance
Lightning Source LLC
Chambersburg PA
CBHW071946100426
42736CB00042B/2252